So that the Butterfly Won't Die

Dear Agnes
with great pleasure
and Friendship
[signature]

TRANSLATED BY KAHTAN MAHBOUB

Cracow, 3.06.202[illegible]

Hatif Janabi

So That the Butterfly Won't Die (Selected Poems)

Translated by: Kahtan Mahboub

United Kingdom
60 Blakes Quay
Gas Works Road
RG3 1EN
Reading
United Kingdom
info@dararab.co.uk
www.dararab.co.uk

First Edition 2022
ISBN 978-1-78871-084-8

دار عرب للنشر والترجمة
DAR ARAB FOR PUBLISHING & TRANSLATION

Text Design by: Nasser Al Badri
Cover Design by: Hassan Almohtasib
Photo credit: Evie S./Unsplash

Contents

Mirrors of Bright Vision in Hatif Janabi's Poetry

"I'm from a land muter than a stone,

harder than the death's sigh in a dying's mouth."

Hatif Janabi is a gifted, innovative poet with bright vision and witty, philosophical mind. He enjoys a flawless, tender heart. His nostalgia for his bereaved homeland and his love for humanity and freedom are unequivocally unbridled. I say these words with confidence because I have known Hatif Janabi and shared with him a happy and bitter life for half a century. The love of poetry, liberty, and our savagely brutalized country has been our spiritual guide and common dominator.

Beautiful, original poetry needs no introduction. However, my experience, as a reader, led me to conclude that understanding and connecting with the poet's backgrounds, ideas, and subject matters could lead to a greater perception and appreciation of his poetry. Translating Hatif Janabi's poems brought me closer to him in spirit and heart; that, at one point, I thought he took the words from my mouth and wrote whatever I wished to write but didn't. Justifiably, my poetry shares numerous images, metaphors, similes, and themes with his. We are both the children of one tragedy, one destiny, one exile, as we share the same hopes and dreams. Hence, I would like to introduce poet Hatif Janabi through this prelude and these selected poems, which I chose from eight volumes of Arabic poetry to our English readers. Then, I will delineate the poet's views on poetry, leaving his poems' literary analysis to a future opportunity or other critics.

Hatif Janabi is uneasy poet to read or fathom passingly. His poetry is as perplexing as his deep vision and wild imagination. Yet, whatever comes from the heart reaches the heart, and I'm honored to undertake such a challenging endeavor not only to translate a first-class, world poet, who happened to be my intimate friend, putting a hold on my literary works for a year and a half, but to resolve any ambiguities and riddles a reader may face with such deep, profound, and sometimes, dark verses. Working on Hatif Janabi's poems, I kept telling him, even in my sleep, you can't fool me Hatif; I know the dimensions of your tidings and toils and will unveil the perplexities and the molecules of your hidden treasures and secrets.

Hatif Janabi and I lived sweet-bitter experiences throughout a long and tragic journey since we found ourselves poets and dormmates, a half century ago, in our sophomore year at the University of Baghdad. Hatif was studying Arabic literature; I was studying English. We were poor, like many other students, but we behaved like princes and millionaires' sons in our neatness and prudence. To put it in his words, "We knitted the stars and the dreams at night and appeared in prophets' status at day." We lived in Al-Waziriya, a pretty and affluent quarter in the suburbs of Baghdad, surrounded by exuberant, rich houses with gardens of roses, gardenias, datepalms, nightingales, and Mercedes and Ferraris, no comparison to poverty-stricken Najaf, Hatif's hometown, and trodden, marshy Maysan, mine. During our stay in this dorm, we walked together to school in the morning, met often in the evenings at my room, (I was the only student with a private room for two years,) and had several poetry readings and discussions about Arabic and English literature. Once, I verbally translated Shakespeare's sonnet "When in Disgrace..." to him while I studied for my homework. We also were privileged to have hot water, and the electricity never interrupted. We lived very quiet, peaceful life. We didn't know, at the time, we these were the happiest days of our lives.

At the beginning of May,1972, before graduation, Hatif Janabi and I participated in the yearly poetry competition held by the University of

Baghdad. I listened to him reading, for the first time, an odd poem, different from any other I had ever read or listened to in Arabic literature. I was surprised even though I had been studying Blank Verse, Free verse, and prose poems, and other untraditional forms and styles of English poetry, like his, for many years. However, Hatif Janabi's poem in the competition fell like "dew to the pasture," as Neruda said, causing an uproar. He connected with the audience of more than two thousand listeners. "People are even comb's teeth," Hatif Janabi quoted the Qur'an to build his poem. "No difference among green, red, or yellow." His simple message, I still remember, called for equality, justice, and fraternity, bringing him fame and recognition overnight; that, a few days later, the Union of Iraqi Writers invited him to read his poem to its audience at its green lawns.

My reading was before the last, for our names were alphabetically ordered. When I took the stage and looked around, my poet friends Hatif Janabi, Nabil Yassin, Abdul Illah Al-Yasseri, (Zahir Jezani and Khaldoon Jaweed, English major,) had reasonably disappeared, unconcerned with the first prize winner. My classical poem, "Why Staying in Baghdad,"[1] coated with venomous honey, was more daring and provocative than all of theirs. Thus, that pleasant spring evening, Hatif Janabi and I were both marked as the most dangerous amongst the poets in the country by the Intelligence Bureau, the *Amin*, secret agents of the Ba'ath Party which usurped power four years earlier and had already begun their pogrom, cleansing any opposition or dissent. After graduation, Hatif and I said goodbye and separated. I thought I wouldn't see him again for a long time.

Our alumni were the first to be drafted to serve a year in the military according to a new decree issued by the ruling Ba'ath Party. On October first, I found myself a soldier in a military training camp in Najaf, [See the Camp's Letter] Hatif Janabi's small hometown, but my friend was nowhere to be found. I thought he was sent to a different training center. After two months of back-breaking, tormenting, horrendous training, sleeping in hotel rooms paid by our meager savings, joined by unbearable hunger and desert frigid weather, [We were still in our summer clothes, only a shirt, when the severe winter of December approached,] the soldiers and I suffered immensely, reaching physical, financial exhaustion, and tragic desperation.

At the beginning of December, betrayed by a distant cousin, one of my two roommates in the hotel, I was sadistically tortured and imprisoned ten days for my poem *The Sultan's Doves.*[2] After my release, Hatif Janabi sought to see and console me. He was trained in the same camp and lived home, but with seven thousand graduates, it was almost impossible to find one another. Hatif and I had a hearty discussion, concluding that Iraq was no longer suitable for poetry or living. From then on, to stay alive, we had to deny being poets. If we ought to write poetry and enjoy our freedom, we had to desert our dear homeland. In fact, we reached this decision simultaneously six months earlier before our poetry readings in our senior year. We both faced severe harassments, and later, more than once, I was targeted by an assassin. In retrospect, if Hatif and I remained eight more years in Iraq, we, most certainly, would have been executed like many of our friends, colleagues, and relatives. Nevertheless, I spent the ten days of my imprisonment agonizing from my wounds and burned arm's excruciating pain, meanwhile writing another, classical poem. However, no one would hear or see my poetry again as long as I was in Iraq.

When I found Hatif Janabi sitting beside me in the military truck taking us to the Sixth Tank Battalion in the forlorn and harsh southern desert of Basra to serve the remaining nine months of our military service, I was confident that we were banished in our own country. General (K. A. D,) my adversary, the poem's inspirer, who tried and sentenced me, exacted his vengeance. The Six Tank Battalion was an ideologist, dogmatic institute, one of the most organized and government loyal in the country. In this camp, where it reaches subzero temperatures in the early mornings of winter and 110 degrees in the summer, Hatif Janabi and I agonized tremendously. We had very little money. I chose to live in a rented room, outside the camp, an hour away, preferring virtual starvation, to be "far from the madding crowd." Hatif stayed in the camp. We spent eight hours a day together, training and teaching illiterate soldiers in the school we initiated, reading the rest of the time.

We were aware of the causes of our exile to this foreboding desert. The heinous months of winter passed painfully but peacefully. At the end of July, with two months to end our service, the Sixth Battalion relocated, in tents' camp, for war exercises, closer to Kuwait. It was a desolate desert, infested with snakes, scorpions, and unmerciful sandstorms. Hatif Janabi, two other graduates, and I were left behind for sixty harsh and brutal days to guard the barracks, around the clock. We practically famished, foraging for food ourselves in an empty camp. A glass of cold water, during these days, was a luxury. The Six Battalion never thought of our well-being. I was acquainted with the commander of the War School, a half mile away, but my dignity prevented me from seeking his help. We endured unimaginable misery, but not as dire as the civil-war tormenting, severe conditions yet to experience in our second, unexpected, reserve draft which lasted another year. This time our division was North, in the mountains. The vicious civil war ended. I was appointed a teach of English in a high school in my home province, Maysan. Hatif was sent to teach Arabic in the northern city of Kirkuk where I visited him during the summer for the last time in Iraq.

Hatif and I were very lucky to escape the third service during the Iranian-Iraqi War which lasted ten years for the men born the same year as we. As soon as the opportunity matured, we both escaped overseas. Hatif smuggled himself through Turkey to Warsaw, Poland, where he received a grant from the University of Warsaw to finish his M.A. and Ph.D. After graduation, Dr. Hatif Janabi pursued his academic, literary work and teaching, eventually receiving his Polish citizenship. I was luckier, having been admitted to the University of Michigan, Ann Arbor, after great feats and sacrifices, the government permitted me to travel to the US, in the fall of 1976, even with severed diplomatic relationships, under heavy financial penalties, guaranteed by my brothers, to return to Iraq upon finishing my Ph.D. After my departure, I lost touch with my friend, Hatif Janabi. I didn't know what happened to him.

Eighteen years later, I located Hatif Janabi through a poem he published in a magazine. We resumed our friendship and correspondence. A few months later, I obtained a fellowship for him from Indiana University, Bloomington, as a vising scholar. He reached me in Pittsburgh in August 1993 to start his American experience of teaching Arabic and learning English. [See Departure] He already had a Ph.D. from Warsaw University in Comparative Drama and Middle Eastern Studies. With the help of a friend, who translated his Arabic poems to English, the University of Arkansas, in 1996, published *Questions and Their Retunes,* a collection of Hatif' Janabi's early poems, winning the first prize among the translated collections of poetry for that year.

Hatif Janabi and his poetry are the outcome of all previous tragedies and misfortunes. Reading his poems in Arabic, I couldn't escape his powerful imageries, rare metaphors, bright visions, melodramatic tantrums, and always bold, enlightening challenges. Hatif Janabi's poems are new in forms and subject matters; rich with the beauty of nature, animals, fish, insects, love of life in its physical and spiritual dimensions, death, existence, destiny, and alienation, to name a few. His poems defy evil in all its shapes and defend human rights, especially those of the victims of religious fervors and radicalizations: the minorities in Iraq and the Arab World, the underdogs, and women's rights.

During his forty-four years residency in Poland and other places, this Nomad, vagabond poet vigorously integrated, forging great ties with the Polish and European societies, cultures, literary movements, and organizations, leaving his marks, influenced by them as well, writing and translating in two languages, as he was influenced by Arabic culture and its rich, ancient literary heritage. Hence, his rewarding experiences of living outside his country, moving from Iraq to Algeria, to Poland, to the United States, and finally England, visiting many Asian, African, and European countries, served him well and helped him immerse in world cultures and literatures, coming out with a unique vision, global perception, and diversity. His innovations, therefore, weren't limited to his poetic form, but included a variety of universal subject matters on which I concentrated in my translations.

Hatif Janabi's form of poetry, which he called "the renewable rhythmic poem" is similar to Blank Verse, or "prose poem" written in 'prose style rather than verse, but contains the characteristics of poetry, such as rhythm, meter, language play, and a focus on thought and image rather than plot and character.' Hatif Janabi also used short narratives in his invaluable "metered poems," which end up mostly in Free Verse in my English translation. Others prose poems were also translated in Free Verse or Blank Verse. Adopting this form of poetry, Hatif Janabi revolted against traditional, classical Arabic Poetry of the strict forms of rhyme and rhythm, and rebelled against the Free Verse, which was newly adopted from English, three decades earlier. Thirdly, Hatif Janabi, in his new form of the "Renewable Rhythmic Poem," challenged Arabic language itself. But before I discuss these three subjects, I need to mention that poet Hatif Janabi wrote and still writes occasionally classical poems and Arabic Free Verse, excelling in these forms as well.

Although I'm an avid admirer of classical poetry, Free Verse, and Blank Verse, in which I have been writing for fifty years and still write, I stand with Hatif Janabi for rejecting these forms, and for adopting his new unique form of the "rhythm poem," or the "metered poem" for the following reasons. Traditional poetry, even with its esthetic beauty and harmonious melodies, restricts the poet and limits the horizon of his imagination by its very firm and rigid rules of forms, rhymes, rhythms, and syntax. Hatif Janabi says, "It belongs to ancient ages and eras that can't contain present heartbeats and visions." He believes that its forms "became captives of their own, hard to implement to express humane, universal horizons, preventing the gifted from exploring his talents and visions."[3]

Hatif Janabi might be a little severe in his punitive judgement, but I concur that this demanding literary genre of poetry might have reached its capacity and limits in our modern times, and not many poets could excel in it. It demands extraordinary talent. The historical literary culture produced only one or two great poets each millennium such as Al-Mutanabi, 9th century, and Al-Jawahiri, 20th Century. Writing in this arduous form, I know, first-hand, how challenging it could be. A poet needs perpetual time, patience, and uninhibited imagination, abiding by the rules of its numerous rhymes and rhythms, which we call "seas," and still harder, the Arabic syntax. Writing in this form, a few Arab or Persian poets were immortalized writing only one orphan poem in their lives. The easiest way to define this kind of poetry is to compare it to the classical music of Mozart or Beethoven, for example.

Hatif Janabi also abandoned the Arabic Free Verse which is still popular, and some Arab contemporary poets write in it. This form shares an intimate relationship with its mother form, the classic. "Its poetic qualities of rhyme and rhythm," Janabi says, "prevail over the prose in it" though it allows the poet to change the frequency of meter or rhythm requirements or restrictions and puts no limits on the length of the lines or verses. Hatif Janabi's form of the "rhythmic poem" sacrifices all previous musical and conventional rules for the sake of profound meaning, unhindered imagery, and freedom of expression. Even though he prefers the "renewable rhythmic poem" to the Free Verse and Classical Poetry, the poet is fully aware of the disparity between poetry and "prose poem," comparing their differences to a horse and a camel. The horse, he says, "represents the vigor and tenacity of poetry while the camel represents its prose and narration."

Moreover, to avoid visibility and simplicity, which Hatif Janabi resents, and to give his poem its momentum of keeping the rhythm, he provokes, to my dismay and torture, as a translator, the traditional structure of the Arabic sentence which puts the verb first or second, but not after the object, at the end of an appositive, restrictive or nonrestrictive clause, or a prepositional phrase. In many of his poems, Hatif Janabi does exactly that; he puts the verb or the subject last in the sentence, causing confusion or misunderstanding, but, eventually, an avid reader will figure it out; and when I translated, I had to reconstruct his sentences to simplify the English poems giving them a new spirit in the new language.

That is how Hatif Janabi's uniqueness and rare talent forges itself. He is modernized, learning, and borrowing from all cultures and literatures to create the invisible and to come with a vibrant poem of his own albeit he doesn't claim to be the first. He is smart too, for he knows that this kind of poetry, prose like, is easy to translate, lush in meaning, imagery, and metaphor, no match to the stoic and rigid traditional, classical Arabic poetry, which would lose its value and beauty in translation, or even the still restricted Arabic Free Verse, but not necessarily more exciting, enhancing, or inviting. Eliminating the artistic qualities of musical rhythm and rhyme, which are integral trends of classical Arabic poetry and Free Verse, Hatif Janabi comes with a solid, concentrated, deeper and richer poetry full of symbols, metaphors, and allusions. His rare virtues and uninhibited imaginations give his poetry a third dimension which is the core of advanced, concrete poetry, needing a second or a third reading to match his fast, metaphorical strides. Hatif Janabi is a prudent, calculating, witty poet, with rare talent and wild ingenuity.

Kahtan Mahboub, Ph.D.

Professor of World Literature

Rochester, Michigan,

March 24th, 2019

1. Kahtan Mahboub, *The Sultan's Doves*, "House of Literary Treasures," Beirut, Lebanon, 1996.

2. Kahtan Mahboub, *Songs for the Morning Rose*, "Al-Meda Press," Damascus, Syria, 2000.

3. Hatif Janabi, "Studies in Rhythm Poems"

Misunderstanding

Spring is late this year with no meaning or cause.
I even forgot myself among the scattered leaves of autumn.

In my homeland, spring is summer's twin;
winter is autumn's neighbor.
We said, life expands and shrivels.
An oasis, the villains transformed into an arid wasteland.
Spring shouldn't disappear like water in the sand.

Is it plausible to say this is a forest without trees?
These shores, filled with sands and oysters,
have no sea to contain their tides.
No clouds, stars, or a sun gleam on the bloom of their cheeks?
Do seasons have a god or a comet to paint their destinies?
Are we meant, my wife, Adam, his dog, and I,
to wear our green clothes,
waiting for a visible or invisible, cunning scene?

As soon as I snip a bud from the branch,
I behold a tear flowing over the bark,
swiftly drying in its place.

Spring is too late this year;
a life lost on its way to burgeoning.

Warsaw, May 23, 2012.
Translated: March 2019 ,9

The Poet

Fascinated by light and darkness,
by a dagger delighted by misery,
by tempest, devastation, and resonance,
by a ferocious beauty,
the alligator, the seal poet
sleeps and awakens, dreaming of words.

The dead bury his voice.
The newly born desecrate his grave,
and, there is no other means
but to stride.

The stone poet,
echoes.
The captivated poet
endures.

2-22-1997

Translated 2-8-2019

Poland's Cup

Take whatever you can
of the sparrow's shine,
the flower's crown,
bathing in the light's pond.
Take the milk of youth, the rounding of the night's breast,
all you wish, free to choose.
I was too adamant to let the air enter my lungs,
twisting the wind's arm,
pouring down the valley's mouth.
My inhales were irregular.
I was without a cover or a shield.
The tide dragged me, the wind gnawed me.
Take!
Your turn has arrived.
I harvested of you the unimaginable;
my spirit liquified in your plants, over your rocks.

Despite the poverty,
you filled my words with elegance, my nights with joy.
And I will fill your cup,
whenever it dries,
with the remainder of my blood.

Jablonna, 3-23-2018

Translated: 2-7-2019

So That the Butterfly Won't Die Inside Me

I dig a hole in the oak of poetry
and open the volcano's mouth
so that the grass burgeons and the roses prickle.

I write so the light, at the tunnel's end, won't die.
The loaf cheers the glory of the blood spilled around it;
the stones have a savor and color;
the flowers have the kiss's weight.

I write so the friend won't die forever;
no tree bends or bud withers;
no datepalm sinks in the landfill of oblivion,
no ink or rain or spring dries;
no man despairs,
or a lover's prayer goes unheard.

I write to tell the wind,
"I'm your brother in storm,
the igniter of the first spark,
the keeper of thunder
the guard of the trail."

I write so the words won't be buried;
the valiant vision won't disappear
in the distraction of sight;

the butterfly won't die inside me;
the nightmare of doubts won't sweep the dream.

I write so that no innocent be slain;
no sinner be stoned;
no child dies from explosion;
no living-dead are mutilated;
no other meaning for water than life;
nor to be like the caves' inhabitants
or a rotten shoe riddled by the roads.

I write so darkness won't be day.
Babel drinks from the hand of light;
the river continues to run to the fields and the plains;
its marks are on the mountains, its glitter among the clouds.

I write so my mother's prayer and father's praise
be the stars' hymn and the clouds' plea;
the invisible be seen, the inaudible be heard,
and the untouchable be touched.

I write to beseech God, "Give me Your email;
let us frankly talk,
to fathom the savor of dialogue and grievance
without a mediator or a spy."

I write so inhalation and exhalation have a meaning,
a purpose in life,
the beloved to have a statue higher than the mountains.

I write so that no seeker is humiliated;
no flower wilts.
You'll be me; I'll be you
as big as air, water, and food.

I write so that the wing will be as spacious as its dream,
the light will be present, in the might of its guardian,
floating in the open space, in us, around us.

I write to be me.

Warsaw, June 8, 2011

Translated, Ventura, Florida Dec. 27, 2017.

A Casual Meeting with a Soldier Returning from the Iraqi War

Carriages of love, bequeathed to the ax,
pass incessantly, bearing man's inheritance from death.

Bum- Bum-Bum
Bum-Bubbbum-
The vicious king died; the nightingale and the magician arrive to arbitrate.
They said, welcome wise gods, the beleaguered from the jungle,
the cave's people to the last drop of love in the wilderness.
Bum Bum-
The curtains of the dropped in the yellow bile;
the morning, prided by feathers, falling from the night's wing.

A dream- sand / dum-dum duddum
How wide is the hate's wasteland; how narrow are the grave's walls?
They departed; only the spark of lightning, from the wolf's eyes,
remained guarding the wind's gates.

"Do you know me in this snow?
The forest's shade follows me all my life;
the ice statue
scatters my dreams like white flakes.
How wretched I was, can't fathom this from that;
even the bare trees morphed to be of my enemies.
The sand is my *Imam*.
The wit is a discarded shoe in the desert's sand.

How can the pouring rain unmercifully peck a human's eye?
A bird hates a field,
the flowers dream of the Creator's scent?

Do you know God is my friend?"

Which one? What God?

"How often He hovered over me,
stood between me and an angel that can only be overpowered by Him.
This God of the seven gates and Babel."

Welcome to the planter in my field,
thriving from my branches.

If God wasn't my friend,
you won't see my heart entranced by this scene
while the past glowers at me.
Ah, how vengeful were his eyes?
It was about to insert me a finger in a sock.

For God's sake, don't mock the roses' memory!
The vain death is harsher than the mightier one of us
who is hiding behind the mask, with his sickle dripping blood.
The drum is in front of me, and the infanticide flute shivers
between the lips."

Are there two Gods:
of the desert,
and the grass?

Let us toast the latter.

The raucous dawn's voice arrives.
The star is dangling by dusk.
Bum, bum,
Let us drink
to the health of humanizing the animate."

Yablona, June 30, 2009
Translated, February 19, 2019

This Is Not My God

The God,
whose claws
they sought,
is drowned
by the details of a waning fight.

The God,
for whom
I search,
since eternity,
is present
in the spacious horizon and beyond.

His sun never sets.
His darkness glows.
The God,
for whom they searched,
is not
mine.

Warsaw, Dec.7th, 2008

Translated: February 19, 2019

The Rose's Rounding Before its Bloom

The distances can be trekked by a foot or a bird,
or the glittering of the keen scythe resting at the right shoulder
of the angel, masked by gloom.

Spring is approaching.
Don't mock the rounding of the rose before its bloom,
nor the old man's steps, leaning on autumn's cane.

Imagine, I hold both the rues and the camphor,
a bouquet of flowers and a dark suit,
extending my hand to shake this and that,
then, stealthily, I pierce the needle of afterlife
in the prey's heart.

Imagine the distance,
whose lighthouse was the insight,
during the night's daze and the dawn's beat,
its steps turned firewood
in a stranger's hearth.

The mute stone may remain silent
to the last drop of water.
Afterward,
the distance fades
between the contradiction and it.

Hence, tranquility becomes the most dominant,
by which even the drum tumbles and fall.

I wished to trek the short and the long distance
at the same trail,
but the scene petrified me.
When I hoped to recount my life's single feat,
I found my blood, drop by drop,
falling behind,
over the sand,
and the wind erases its trail.

Warsaw, Feb. 29, 2008
Translated: 9-20-18 2:17 A.M

Suggestion

She stood gazing at my face,
saying:
"The phone can be heard; I intend to whisper.*
Your name will be prettier if it is different. "

"How lovely," I replied.
"A woman chooses the symbol of my affection.
Give me another life, my lady,
I will throw my name under your shoe."

Jablonna, June 30, 2009

* The poet's name Hatif means a phone in Arabic.

Reading

Do I see
the sea reindeers
or the piranhas of the field?
Is that, shedding her gown, a cloud?
Or that, raining, is a forest?
Is that, who writes poetry, a crocodile,
or a poet who swallows the fish?
Is that you who eats from my God's hand?
and, who kicks him, is mine?
Don't say this darkness is from my light,
and that light is from your opaqueness.
Don't say what you see is a dream,
and what is happening is a mere book
the winds scan,
the sands read,
in your absence.

Birmingham, June 14, 2018
Translated: February 21, 2019

Writing with Chinese Ink

One: Chinese Women

They work, day and night.
When winter arrives,
they sit in the sunflowers' place, flickering like a flame.
Each wears two earrings of lotus,
brightening her cheeks' dimples.
They harvest flowers during the summer
for men to gather their leaves in autumn.
When they retire to bed,
they half-shut their eyes,
leaving a guarding smile on their lips.

Beijing, China 10-14-2019 - Translated: 2-5-2021

Two: A Conversation with a Chinese

I pondered in her face, descended to her depths,
and read uttering silence in her expressions,
a hesitation of two waves, in her looks,
before they descend to the seabed.
I whispered, "From where are all these pearls?
which way will take me to their charm?" my Lady.
She gazed away lest the light unveils her shyness.
"The sole canoe was wrecked, my Lord," she replied.
"Only voyaging by the boat of waves, thunders, and lightnings was left."

Beijing's International Airport, 10-15-2019 - Translated, 10-13-2019

Three: My Father's Blue Eyes and the Wall of China

"Father" I said, after silence fell,
"Have you seen a cloud ram a mountain's top?"
"Have you seen a child light a candle from the smile of the moon?" he replied.
We laughed together and shared a cup of wine.
In our homeland, we have no sheath but the stars;
no substance but to cross life's ocean on a dolphin's back,
dreaming that the slippery canoe wouldn't skid into the whale's mouth;
that the elements would sink us to the depth
or lift us higher than China's dream and her Wall.

Suddenly, at the world's midnight,
the azure of my father's eyes' glittered,
and in the presence of a comet,
the lids rapidly closed their doors.

Still transcending the universe,
dreaming of the Wall, cuddling the clouds,
wondering how Man converses with the deities,
climbing the stair of eternity,
then succumbs to build his nest
between the sand and the mud?

Beijing, China 10-13-2019 - Translated: 2-5-2021

Four:Tofu

I touched him, caressed his beard, then bent over his frail body.
His statue wasn't merely a stone.

His vascular veins and heart's pulses extend from my limbs' ends
to the last shiver in my body and inhale in China's blood.
Oh, wise, don't say more than what you left,
or look back at the past in whose wisdom you were baptized.
Life's distance is a drop of water between the roots and the leaves.
I found you Mutanabi's equal.
In *Gilgamesh*, I read your ancestors,
grasping the spark of creation,
releasing it in the houses, the fields, the streets, and memories.
This bail you carry is an undiminished light's fountain, a well of wisdom.
I, a stranger, who never felt lonely among your descendants,
abluted with its water.

I bid him farewell at the beat of the last sentence he uttered at my hearing:
"Don't fear darkness.
Follow the light of poetry.
The lightning's spark omits the footprints."

Tshingdo, China 10-10-2019 - Translated: 2-5-2021

Five: To Lee Pie: The god of Poetry

Numerous are the gods of poetry.
They write on sand and mud,
on the pages of clouds and rains.
Several select an untrodden road,

greeting perfidious shades,
or hang a white rag on a broken branch.

I espied him busy with his vintages' barrels,
dipping the feather of poetry in life's inkwell,
then grasp it a flame from the blood of his chalice,
drawing it with the sparks of tornedoes and hurricanes.
I asked him, "How much time lapses between the lifting of the cup
and the first drop's collision over the poetry's rock,
for the fountain to spring and the dream's first desire to forge,
nourishing the meadow of words?
How much time lapses between a trip and another
for the curtain to slip from darkness and the dawn shines?
Tell me Lee Pie:
What is the difference between the flask's mouth
and this flourishing lip of which the lover's blood flows?"

I beheld the flowers filling the hat.
The golden ray covers the estray body in the Yangtze River
while Pie, still in his departure, ignites his perplexed soul.

The House of Du Vow, China , 10-10-2019
Translated 2-26-21

From the Memory of Cities: Birmingham

In Birmingham, the clouds delude the sky,
barter roles between crossing and absence.
The wind plays with the straw,
autumn with the shroud.

I walk near ancient buildings, crowned with hats.
We too swap roles.
I behold ruins, reconstructed teeth,
bewildered eyes, and an unfinished biography.
Rain whips me with the sins of others.
Oh, vision, don't be coy; we are all visitors.
I beseech the pubs, the lightnings, the memories.
I march; the canal takes me to a past
when, barefoot, I used to trek near the edges of creeks.
The farthest I went, the sticker my shoes became.

The Bridges lead me to museums and bookstores.
I grudgingly greet two currency-exchangers.
They pretend to count money or talk by phone.
"I'm Hatif, too," I screamed,*
but a plane interrupted the sequence.

Dum, dum, dudum, weeeezzzzz, bum, bum, bubum,
my wife hides under the table, shivering of fear.
Ah, it's the ugly Gulf War.

Then, she awakens from her nightmare.

Birmingham isn't any other city.
I've seen here what likened rockets carrying distilled water.
Baghdad also has a sky, golden domes, and bridges.

I shake a trunk, then rapidly forget my share of the fruit.
I gaze at the golden dome;
how often has it saved me from bewilderment?

In the City Centre, I'm the blind led by an insight.
I see musicians, beggars, mysterious claimers.
enticing or threatening, waving their Book,**
flickering, thundering, foaming
in the name of a god who shakes the clouds' tail
until their tears roll down over the idlers' heads.

Ah God, do You recall, like me,
what is falling over the heads in Babylon?
What did Ophelia say on the death trip?
I invite You, for a picnic across time and space.
Look at this book about the Tower of Babel,
and that decorated one about Al-Rashid's harem and Scheherazade.
Don't frown, oh, Grand!
We will read together a final, more useful subject:
"How to Establish a Successful Business?"
Oh, Great, don't say Your humble slave is a miser.

I'll invite You over un-Iraqi cake.
If You desire a drink to quench the thirst,
to help You forget this ingratitude.

Birmingham is a stranger like me;
its spirit inhabits the storm.
Even its birds and winds have a scent.
"Where is Shakespeare and his folks?" I ask.
"They live in its bricks," they reply,
"in its castles, its leaves, its women,
among the lines we read, even outside its boundaries.
Whoever sleeps in his bed doesn't own any of its walls."

The heavy guest, the rain, chases me.
I shelter by the City Library shelves.
I watch a romantic movie and Star Wars.
Birmingham sleeps now.
The shade alone observes the light,
and I still guard the flocks of clouds.

Birmingham, May 25, 2015.
Translated: 12-20-18 Ventura, Florida.

*The phone is called Hatif in Arabic
** The Qur'an or the Bible

Invitation

After now, I won't invite anyone
to my house, inhibited by ghosts.
My lock is rusty.
Whoever used to greet me is a pig.
My neighbors are rats.
I won't invite their daughter for fear of the Jinni's king,
sitting behind the door.
I won't invite the dolphin, friend of desolation
or whoever crawls behind the Sultan's shades.
I won't invite whomever is invited to life's luxuries.
Tonight,
I've decided to invite the sea and all its fish,
to take me,
after the party,
to the whale's abdomen
so that I write my life's story
and sing my awaited tune.

June 16, 2014

Revised and Translated: 12-28-18

Languages I Am Not In

I decipher words in which I breathe.
They loathe me, spit in my face; I kick.
They paint me a statue, a stone, a featherless sparrow,
an infidel, an exiled pirate, in deserted islands.
Voices of all colors and tongues
talk of a past of which I'm unaware.
Hands cut a thread of a kite, hanging on to the clouds,
mourned by this lonely child.
In the languages of controversies,
a signature over a cloud,
a blind seeks a lantern.
Words read me; letters, fall from my pocket,
heard by the dead from the dead' mouths.
But the first letter and the next are mixed
in the chaos of searching
for meaning to write oneself outside what is written.

Words I breathe in,
but I'm not the one
who lives in.

Birmingham, January 8, 2015

Brighten My Ways

I stare inside me.
I see shades of dreams in scattered directions,
fish swim in drying aquariums,
and in every road, some contradicting signs.
These dolphins and piranhas know me though I don't.
These butterflies and spiders, prairies and pastures
see me, but I don't.
Another face of the winds, this coarse drum,
the sound arrives from these depths.
"My roars can't save me."
I raise my injured index, waving it right and left.
The skies object; the roots bandage it.
All this pains me.
I stare at this darkness and beyond,
carving bleeding letters on its walls.
I see my index, like an arrow,
sink in a heart that is not mine.
"Oh, God of retribution,
oh, Lord of vengeance,
shine my opaque ways!"

Warsaw, September 28, 2014.

Invisible Letter

Do you believe that I died?
Now, I write from a life after life?
Here, the hands and the glares intertwine.
Even the branch can invite,
then suffocates the wrists
so that the fingers turn green.
A meadow forges in the head; a rose blooms in the heart.
Spring is eternally here; every sign refers to it.
Permanent absence of shape, beauty, and ugliness,
youth equates old age.
Even I write these words
at the sheet of wind and lightning,
to be a seemingly breeze, a rainy cloud, a storm.
Don't be baffled if I live, for a moment,
with half of my heart and one lung.
Don't mourn my departure,
for what we do here is to reaffirm the oxygen's fraternity.

Remember that transparency is a loathsome habit.
The weakest point for a matter is to be obviously clear.

Birmingham, June 12, 1015

Poetry Reading

I intended to delay my visit to Mother's grave.
The sky was hastily spreading its maps.
I suddenly halted at the Twentieth Revolution Square,
where no revolutionaries moan; no guns poised.
I stopped but, due to heavy dust and numerous pedestrians,
I couldn't see the faces well.
The walls and the stones were only witnesses
mending, with the night's nails, the memory of oblivion.
I recalled:
here were erected statues;
now, all departed in congruent with the calendars of years.
The King disappeared; the Brigadier was removed.
The landmarks, the roses, which applauded our success, humbled their heads.
The signs became incomprehensible.
There was swarming to another world.
Even the *Imam* no longer cared;*
perhaps for the lack of time, or the petitioners multiplied.
Everyone goes to his destiny;
the day to its hideout;
the politician to his perfidies;
the poor to the illusory dream of feasts;
the clergymen reap life's rewards and clarify
what remained of myths.

I lonely walked in the cemetery's road,

searching long in the pockets of dusk.
Finding no one,
I took out this poem and began to rehearse,
touching the hearing of the dead.

Birmingham, Dec. First, 2014

Translated: December 28, 2017, Ventura, Florida.

* *Imam* Ali Bin Abi Talib

Bleeding Heart

"My lady," I hesitantly said,
"What is this misery in your eyes,
the blue carnation covering your lips?
She sighed from her spirit's depths:
"For I waited,
all this life,
with a bleeding heart,
and a hole in my lungs."

Warsaw, May 24, 2012

In Her Eighty

She dreamt of the wedding kiss,
brought a photo from the album,
a tear, as big as eighty years,
descended to her lips.

A Needle

Every day,
she sat at the steps
of her house,
mending her tattered socks,
searching for a memory.
One morning,
she dozed off
while the needle dreamt
between her index and thumb.

Marble Woman

She bathed daily in cold water.
In the summer,
she put cubes of ice
in her bathtub
and rubbed her body with olive oil,
wearing the finest perfumes.
She lived long with a gleaming, tender body.
In respect for her redolent memory,
they put her in a coffin of ice
and wrote on her tombstone:
"Here rests a woman of marble and snow."

How Dark My Heart Was

Suicide

The lover suicides twice.
He cheats once,
and agonizes under the ankles.

Falling

The leaves fall in autumn
to mourn the beauty's death.
Darkness
The truth is the most glittering sword.
The deepest blue
is the sea's eyes.
Darkness is the brightest word.
An arrogant breast
is the highest summit in the world.

Dark Heart

Man's hair grays
to say:
how opaque my heart was?

Laws

Hammurabi decreed his code
so that the tyrant
hangs his revolver over it.

Boredom

Man is born
so that he won't die of boredom,
idle, in his mother's womb.

Misunderstanding

God sent the prophets and the messengers
for a misunderstanding
between Him and mankind.

Intelligence

The wise reasons for decades
to be certain he said a prudent thought.
The idiot repeats every moment:
how clever I am.

Veil

The Muslim woman wears a veils
to tell men:
you are unworthy of seeing me.

Waiting

Patience is the poor's weapon.
Waiting is poverty's worst foe.

Misery

God created Adam
to tell future generations:
I'm the most miserable of you all.

Dumbness

Silence is gold;
hence,
gold has decided to be mute.

Congratulation

The first assassin in history is the man,
for he spilled the woman's blood.
She was the first to congratulate him.

Striptease

The most wasteful of seasons is the summer.
The most generous is spring.
Winter is the stingiest.
Autumn is the least bashful,
for it is always nude.

Sword

The sharp sword
needs a sheath;
the dull sword
has no sheath.

Beauty

The horrid words
need harsher tongues
to be pretty ugly.

Importance

The deficient woman
needs a faultless man;
the imperfect man
needs a woman
who doesn't care for excellence.

Kindness

Beautiful concepts
do not always charm,
for their heart is always kind.

Flute

The man to the woman:
be a guitar.
The woman to the man:
I like the flute more.

Width

Whenever a human's brain shrivels,
his perfidy increases.
When his mind ripens,
his heart widens.

Misconception

The Japanese lady customarily walks behind the man,
for she thinks he is a horse, pulling her.
The man stands in front of the woman,
for he endeavors to look forward.

Dependency

God depended on the prophets.
The prophets depended on mankind.
Man depended on God.

Agreement

The Palestinians and the Israelis
agree on two issues:
they are of the same origin,
and they must prove this
by the weapon's might.

Warsaw, December 1990

Translated 2-19-2019

Between Laughing and Crying

An Eye

Darkness is the eye of the blind.

Eyes

Man has two eyes.
The insightful has three.

Gambling

Don't ever gamble with God.

Competition

The poet, the painter, the musician
are nature's most avid friends
and deadliest competitors.

Danger

The witty coward
is more dangerous than a foolish brave.

Pierced Sack

Beauty, without virtue and compassion,
resembles grain in a pierced sack.

Carriage

The disgraced ruler
is a carriage without a horse.

Pimp

The foolish dictator
is a burden, an unwitty guest:
a pub without wine,
a pimp in a church.

Breathing

The shoe has holes in it to breathe.

Signal

Talkativeness is barking.
Wisdom is a call from the depth;
silence is a beacon.

Cancellation

I cancelled all my trips to the moon.
I am travelling toward the Sun.

Perpetual Silence

If people talk the language of God,
clergymen will be silent forever.

The People of Heaven

There is more than one flaming hope for the people of hell.
There is no hope for the people of heaven.

Perfume

All the perfumes of the world
can't equate a woman in love.

A Threat

Life tells death:
oh, death,
you have no hope, in life, after me.

Gnawing

Death to life:
laugh, laugh, sooner or later,
I will gnaw your heart.

Agony

Woman's breasts are the most symmetrical summits of nature.
The most tormented objects
are man's eyes.

Violation

Nakedness is more elegant than a pierced gown.
A tattered gown is more protective than a sick mind.
An ailing mind is nobler than a debased grace.

Arrogance

Arrogance is a sailing ship
in a sea of sand.

Tyranny

A full pub
is livelier than an abandoned church.
An abandoned church
is safer than a brutal country.

Opaqueness

The torturer:
why do you sigh?
The victim:
This endless lunacy and the gloom.
The torturer:
Craziness glows in the dark.

Letter

Love is an endless book
with only few words.
I gift my life to you.

Sincerely,
Love.

Two Lips

The mouth has two lips
so that the words won't slip down.

Horn

The Arabs say:
The earth sits at a bull's horn
because she is feminine.

Pittsburgh and Bloomington, Indiana, July-August 1994

Translated: June 26, 2019

Polishing

When he heard of Michael Jackson,
he was a handsome lad,
polishing his shoes repeatedly,
combing his hair with imported gel and a side spit.
He never worried about dust,
nor the rarity of dancing in a Bedouin society.
He wrote poetry.
The critics and the publishers disenchanted him,
advising:
"Be merrier, more feminine in your poetry and life!"
He began dancing stealthily,
a traditional and a western dance,
gathering the shells of his disappointments,
liking every odd in the dictionaries.
In a certain moment,
he felt a stomachache,
a shiver flowing in his imaginations and veins.
Since then, he kept in touch,
polishing his verses
with a shoe brush,
scattering his oysters on the road.

Translated: September 2018

Iraqi Visits

One:

"Come, Gilgamesh, be my chosen groom!
If you enter our house, the steps and the rails
will kiss your feet," Ishtar said to Gilgamesh.

Tattered clothes are discarded on the roads.
Dusts cover the trees. Empty cups,
dreams howl day and night.
A pear doesn't know if it contains camphor or desertion's savor.
A shoe chases me, stitches my body.
Do you, my shadow, see, like me, mute gods, hanging over the doors?
Talk to me, my semblance,
is Babel crying behind the hill, or this is the shepherd: the wolf?
Ishtar was only a stone in a decadent wall?
Awake me, lest my night trails my steps.
The opaqueness of the nights' people suffices me.
Awake me from the slap of the freedom's crocodile
behind the landfills of Babel and the slaughterhouse.
Tell me, Marduk,*
is God's light without lines,
and the flame is the god Shamash?
Should we invite Gilgamesh to slaughter Humbaba again,
or build another Babel from clay inside the riverbed?
My spirit is a ruptured shoe.

Where are the rivers, the paradises of gods who betrayed us?
Where are the towers and the carvings on the walls?
Were they meant to crumble over the crucified body?
I never entered a house and the step or the rail didn't kiss my foot.
Like shadows, I wished to pass by a lion seemed to be a captive shade,
in a land in which whose dominance was a tower equal to the Creator's ray.
I didn't enter; wings condescended over me,
and the vision waned,
in a marble statue, which, at dawn, gouged out its eyes forever.

Tell me, my shadow:
"Who is trailing me, you or the assailant?"
"No difference at all," says the shade,
"between the first breast and the other."

Warsaw, September 2, 2011

* Marduk is the Sumerian chief deity in charge of Babylon.

In *Gilgamesh*, Humbaba is the fearsome demon who guarded the Cedar Forest, forbidden to mortals, defeated by Gilgamesh.

Two:

During my swift visit,
after severing my ties to the fountain,
the streets informed me of faces whose features I knew all;
the semblance between the presence and its walls,
the absence and its dreams.
The sand increased that my hand gave up on removing it
from the language's shoe.
My language: I said, I died to resurrect your spirit in me,
in my arduous trip,
through universes that didn't settle without a slaughter:
no convivial tapster in it ever quenched.
Whose cup stirred over its vices;
the tune and the echo equated in its norm.
Have you seen, in life's cemetery, roses I planted
and water I poured over its chest?
Did windows, established behind me, over a moaning drum, were shut down?
Then, the heaven's people finished mending their edifice
after crowning its forehead
with a halo from the glory of the past?

I was searching for a lisp whose beginning I carved over the absence's lock.
The clouds' language wasn't one.
The flags of the flagrant stars were lowered down,
and the truth's candle was smothered.
But the aroma of yesterday and eternity are still emitted from the verses' sound.
The talk, whose inceptive the learned grasped,

was carried away by the winds,
becoming a book, its lines, copied by the storm,
rehearsed by the child, the old man, and the beseecher.

My language, I said,
I'll smash what is optimistic in dictionaries
and scatter the dust over their graves.
I have, over the clouds, towers and icons,
a sun, whose braids I tie to the minarets,
hopeful of the young dawn
and the perplexed nightingale's tweet.

What a wonder?
For a millennium, and the "Salam Valley,"*
reconciles, day and night,
treasuring what the reaper and the farmer earned.

My language, I said,
there is no resemblance to this marriage
between life and ***its*** inhabitants. **
We awaken at the drumbeats and doze off
at the whisper of the unparalleled guard.
My language, I said,
have you seen, like me, the lanterns,
melting, behind the threads of white,
which, a while ago, were combing
the dreamer's lock?

In my anticipated trip to Najaf,
I visited my mother's tomb and the *Imam*'s,
but
I wept for my homeland.

Warsaw, August 31, 2011

Trans. Dec. 2018

* Salam Valley, "Wadi Al-Salam," the largest cemetery in the world, extends for tens of miles in the Najaf desert west of Iraq.

** Wadi Al-Salam: The cemetery.

Three: The Moon Lost Its Way

In my second visit to Iraq,
my stride was alien;
the moon faded in the mirror of my voice.
My dream to visit Irbil Castle was postponed,
faded in the alleys, behind the curves of its walls.
But the bones were buried in the hills and valleys.
If you shouted, the echo would reach you
like a chant rehearsed by thunders.
If you sheltered by the mountainside,
the violets would emerge like a fence,
and the fogs doze off on your eyebrows.
Don't forget the cloud's face or its tears,
or the bracelet of the one who nursed her infant
at the chasm's waist;
whose people were slaughtered,
and dust demised her memory.
Yet, she burgeoned like an orchard over a meadow,
becoming a shrine to which the butterflies, the birds,
and the youths' desires pilgrimage.

That thunder, at the top, wasn't too loud.
It was only the exhales of a God mourning his Kurds
after hearsing his absent, loved ones.*

Warsaw, August 28, 2011
Translated: Dec. 17, 2018

*Hearsing: walking in the hearse or procession of the dead.

Upside Down

To be safe,
whatever you see must be read backward.
The trash doesn't exist;
cleanliness is the devil's work.
Electricity is on an open-ended vacation;
its perpetual presence means sedition.
Sidewalks have no value;
they call for chaos and profit, God's willing,
after signing the false contracts.
They will bring you closer to the resurrection of the "Awaited Mehdi."*
Black is the alternative to the secrecy shield of the passing pornography.
The day has no presence; it is unemployed.
Expertise is an invention of the colonialist;
a hanger of unforgiven faces.
Walking with the whim's cane is a safety ship.
Read whatever you see backward,
except the "Verse of Hypocrisy."**
Read it often and hang it a motto at the Liberation Square!

Oh, strange time?
Oh, God, how many enemies You have?

Najaf, Iraq, August 22, 2015
Translated: Jan.17, 2019

* The Shi'a Muslims believe that the Awaited Mehdi, the Twelfth *Imam*, who disappeared suddenly, will return one day, to govern the world, somehow similar to the second coming of Jesus Christ. (The Translator) ** a verse in Qur'an.

Summarizing

Behold the river cheerfully panting
at the moment of the tide.
The desert dotted by nakedness,
omission inhibits its features.
The bird's peak begs for a dry loaf.
How do the ants open a road where the vision ends?
Is this a "strait path" more transparent than our souls?
Spy the invisible; hear the unheard;
put your fingers in the mouth of the drum;
observe how the horizon wafts.
Then, you will fathom the enormity:
that dusk sees you, but you don't.

Bless the night clad by dawn!
The paper promised by ink,
and the butterfly which copies its colors at the meadow's page.
Bless the roses' pedals, blooded by the crimson's sigh,
creeping to the heart.
Bless the insomniac eyes for gazing at the unknown!
Kiss the flowers' dew at the pistils.
Cheer the wings, fluttering at the branch!
Bless the springs passing you,
attributing behind the mountains!
Glorify each desire, sigh, gasp
the feather tossed by winds with no resolve.

Bless the rainbow as it severs the sky in half!
Kneel to whoever gifts life, from oblivion, without lungs.
Remember, the love of a stone
is more pungent than a foul air!
A spit is prettier than words soiled by perfidy.
The kiss is richer,
more delicious than the treasures of Solomon.
Love is a dream without an end,
a gift that can't be bequeathed or returned.
The "No" is nobler, mightier than 'yes."
This is what the blind hoopoe said
and futility ignored.

Birmingham, Sept. 18-2016
Translated Jan. 10, 2019

Destinies

My letters trip; wires dangle beneath the knees,
in a land abandoned me before the strangers gnawed its face.
My trade is to nip the light from the abyss's lips,
and, with my kiss, tailor the gown of words.
But what does the mouth's swish write over the body?
Between my vision and me stood the brittle of time.
I scratched the skin of meanings by a comet's nails
so that the stars ignite, and the sky's spark creeps into its veins.
For every house a story, every letter has an image,
every word a chisel at the shaving of vision,
a cancer penetrating the air.
Even the wind closed its ears,
waiting for the passing of the storm.

Yablona, Poland, 2-25-2017

Translated, January 18, 2019

Applaud

I applauded long for the trees' branch,
for it resembles life's flag,
for the wing, for it resembles imagination;
for the Earth,
because it is the mother of the sky;
for love since it is the only free giver.
I cheered the stone for it emulates silence.
When I applauded the heart,
it beat, thudded, and throbbed.
And since its first shivers,
I began searching for it
among the flocks of the clouds.

Birmingham 8-18-18

Translated Friday, Feb. 1, 2019

Identities

One: A Homeland

I was born near the river,
and the family's dog,
growing at the horses' beats and shrines' norms.
I became a flute, played by a passing Nomad,
at the hearing of a drum.
I emerged out of the tree's depth,
crossing life's ocean on a stubble,
still oaring in its waves.

I'm from a land muter than a stone,
harder than the death's sigh
in a dying's mouth.

Birmingham. 8-18-18

Two: A Psalm

The air reads me;
its gale documents me.
I enter its bellow,
a lost psalm,
David was searching for.

Three: Roots

I was drunk, listening to the trees' swishing.
They tease my body's branches with their leaves.
I lived in duress like Native Americans with the deer and the eagles.
I studied the book of fortune and fed the ants my bread
until the wolves crawled on to my oasis
that I became a bite between the teeth of dusk.

Four: Face's Geography

Scars on my face
lead the strangers to it,
pushing its leaves to the fields.
The stream, though, runs behind a hill.
Whenever I greet it,
it replies with a murmur.

Five: Hospitality

I loved butterflies,
overwhelming me by their flowers.
When I departed, I found my heart
dangling on a light beam,
between two summits.

Six:Nails

I crossed the borders with one of my lungs.

A tourist snapped and hanged my shade on a bird's wing.
We used to lend each other the sidewalks' smoke.
The roads expanded until I forgot
that I stood in the middle of the shade from the light,
open-handed, crooked-legged
with a little tilted head,
waiting for the winds
to unclothe from me
the nails of the storm.

Seven: Windmill

Life was sand puffed by memories,
thorns and hennas listening to the drumbeats.
Between a night and its noon, the eyelash fell on the grass;
the eyelids were tied to mighty ropes.
Beneath the summit are cottages and pastures over which the eagles hover.
Nearby are tribes of gorgeous dames.
What is yesterday then?
Is it a flag to be raised to judgement day?
And you are, of it, a thread weaved by this time?
How can the yarn invent itself to reweave its rug a second time?
Do you see it, in this season, creating a third road?
Or is it a rock, rolling down from the high sky?
The absent has an excuse like the present has a stab;
waves pushing waves,
a lung inhaling another,
a windmill gazing at the fields
with the eyes of a grindstone.

Eight: My Father

He was more careful than an ant over the details of his life,
cleansing his body, every second, from the days' remains.
A chosen language, protecting the norm and the status.
In this manner, he fought his battles with time.
Whenever he gazed at the mirror, he yelled:
"Is this face someone else's statue or a passing pose?"
Father used to touch his thin mustaches,
near to fondle, with a smile, his genitals, saying:
"Man will be remembered by his deeds."

Before his death,
every generous part of him shriveled.
I watched him glaring at the roof, whimpering:
"I want to go to my home and children.
This wound is getting wider; is there someone to mend?
You, guest, stand up and sew it;
else the clouds will abduct me."
A child, I recall, hitting the page of water with my fist,
Father's hand suddenly emerged among us like a shadow,
preventing the vision between two shores.

In his final days, he began to knock on the door from inside,
calling, tenderly:
"I'm from the people of Babel,
why doesn't the door open?"

What a stupid joke is this,
the night plays,
the wind listens to?

Translated: 2-1-19

Nine: Ruins

Fifty years later,
symbols, scars, and maps, from distant creatures,
marked my face.
Some up-side-down signals, deserts, lines
resembling a gap, left by lightning, in the wilderness.
The most profound are distances the days decoded.
I asked an angel about two eyes, two chasms,
whose depth expanded to the sky.
He was more perplexed than a feather
under the jaw of the winds.

Birmingham, Warsaw 9-20-18 to 10-14-18
Translated: 2-1-2019

Ten: Departure

After bidding Pittsburgh goodbye under rain showers,
and the magic of Al-Mandwee's "Ginza Raba,"*
August was peeling my face by a breeze,
approaching
from the cornfields,

at Bloomington's outskirts.

There, one day, my neighbor told me,
his grandpa lived long among the wolves,
hunting buffaloes and ibexes,
reading, from the palm of thunders, his fortune,
painting with the reindeer's horns,
what he saw coming,
on the face of his tent.
After his grandpa's death, the army hired his talented father
to trail the footprints between Indiana and Ohio.

"After my sudden birth in Texas," he said,
"Father had no more to do,
than paining my still-forming face."

My neighbor glared me and whispered:
"You are my semblance;
your father will depart without recognizing you.
Your fortune is mirrored on your forehead.
I see you recording, with a cloud's feather,
the movement of thunder and lightning,
waiting for the noon star."

Bloomington, Indiana, 12-22-1993
Translated, 2-2-2019

* Poet Al-Mandwee, Kahtan. The poet's host and intimate friend.

** *Ginza Raba, The Treasure of God,* is the sacred book of the Manda'eans.

Eleven: The Winds of America

The winds in Indiana do not resemble those of Chicago,
nor do the winds of Chicago fathom the sky's secrets of New York.
But an invisible thread, even the clouds can't behold,
gradually knits a sail, at the beats of drums.
It looks like a canoe's dream in the sea,
chasing a world,
whose secret can only be fathomed by Moby Dick;
(whose captain hadn't returned yet from invading the seas.)
One day, emerging from dawn,
I was about to sail the world's skies through it,
with two borrowed wings,
penetrating the sunset,
like an arrow passing through its rays.
His dream resembled mine.
I was about to be hooked by the breasts of its sky.

Warsaw, 11-1-2018

Twelve: The Day's Exhale

I asked permission of fields
gathering their colors in butterflies' wings;
whose roads do not betray;
branches do not wither,
cutting some of their leaves.

I formed, from their foliage,
words that cry
in the face of the sky.

Their hand's alphabet is their chisel,
engraving themselves on the clay's surface,
then bake it with the day's exhale.

Dublin, 12-27-18
Translated: 2-2-19

Thirteen: Listening

I listened enough to my shade,
to humankind, and me.
Now, I listen to the wind and lightning,
to the giggle of the stars,
penetrating the skull of wilderness.

Jablonna, 11-7-2018
Translated: 2-5-19

Fourteen: Searching for a Mask

As I read me,
sixty years later,
I can't find
what refers to my past.
Is it a chimney,
in the prairies of Native Americans?
Or a star
at the highest of a mountain's summit?
Is it a sickle

slaying what is in the road
to the grave?

Jablonna, 12-6-17

Fifteen: Restrictions

My entire life,
I've put my hand over my cheek,
a spy in front of my eyes,
a scarf over my neck,
waiting for every part to return
to me.

Sixteen: Fear

Every day, I omit my memory,
to be born again,
waiting for the words
to smell my pen and the inkhorn I prepare.
I fill the lungs, the tongue, with vision
the hearing with the unknown,
for fear of any casualty.
Hence, you see my day
fearing the following one.

Jablonna, 11-17-2018
Translated, 3-12-2019

Three Portraits

Portrait One

Secrecy is of the cover's shield.
We knitted the stars and the dreams at night,
appearing, in the status of prophets, at day.
I talked in this level to myself,
to a plant dangling among the rocks.
Children's innocence veiled my dwelling
in the faculty's resort,
swallowing my ideas for fear of violation:
the coming minus the past;
the sky elevator worked day and night,
not far off from the black mamba of destiny. *

I stretched my hand in the chasm's mouth,
but I have no idea how the last episode was postponed.
I talked alien languages, passed through stages
whose convivial tapsters were the storms and the snows.
I drank and raced the clouds in their discourse.
I saw myself as a dolphin, crossing the seas alone.
The relatives ignored me;
the strangers gifted me.
Betrayed repeatedly, I was unaware
the victim was the hangman.
I starved, but treasured my tattered shoes,

through whose holes I saw
my enemies.

I adored all women and flowers,
loved my friends and the skies
without aim;
my dog was the most faithful of all.

I didn't have one god;
I beheld my god in every deity.
Wherever I headed, I saw a vulture, hovering,
deep valleys, horizons, extending without mercy.
Through the prairies, I screamed,
"Oh prairies,"
the echo greeted me, praaa-irrr-iiies.

In the party of the blinds and the deceived,
I found my likeness divided between a drum and a guitar.
I gathered what I could of sounds and strings,
returning, from the other world to my family.
They were happy to see me;
"Oh, Father of Adam," they said,
"We have changed so much.
This era is unfit for honest living.
Whoever lucky died.
Who lived, randomly lived.
What about you, Father of Adam?"

I pointed to a hole in the wall.

'Home is where my spirit is," I used to say.
The tilted minaret is the string of light,
to my maiden sister's hair,
to my father who no longer recognizes me,
recalling his days among the flocks of clouds.

I ushered to the wrinkles in my forehead,
put my hand over my heart,
panting, sighing,
then departed like a train
leaving the station.

I've never seen in my life
a more profound dialogue.

Birmingham, 4-22-2015

* The mamba is the deadliest and fastest snake in Africa.

Portrait Two

My sleep interrupts that I couldn't abandon what awakening gave me
of hearing, scratching me, an outlook imprisoning me inside one vision:
wicked roads, deceiving lights, martyred lovers in the name of love,
news of the dead without a cause, multiplying sins,

and the living standing in rows at locked doors,
seeking anyone to open.
Someone retreats; I don't know where.
Are these signals observing us from outer space?
Or fighting meteors, shadows we don't comprehend?
"What is this shade among the trees," I yelled,
"Is this the neighbor?"
I thought my bed in Birmingham prolonged the night,
but the days, in Warsaw, shortened too.
The sun, though laughing, was heading west, and, on the farthest corner,
sits an old drunkard begs and hallucinates:
"Zero minus zero," this black and white.
A coachman spikes me in the name of oblivion,
open pages that, for ages, hadn't been read.

Insomniac, I decided to walk at night,
outside my shadow, to spend the siesta in beds of love.
Even the kiss began to weave me at unknown times.
I shut the sun's eastern and western curtains
which have photos filled with flowers and butterflies,
crossing an open-breasted river
with high shoulders,
receding clouds behind the hills.

Without the charming mermaids in front of the water,
and some deer, the scene would've been, a forlorn kingdom, from far.
I shut my eyes over an endless meadow.

That, on the other day,
I heard no more than knocks and chirpings
of two beaks, over the house's glass.
A life may be born over the branch near the window,
in the shade of flowers,
not far away from the exhales
of the open-mouthed piranhas.
Roses shade me inside my house.

Birmingham, 5-5- 2015
Translated, Ventura, Florida Dec. 27, 2017

Portrait Three

I was born in the countryside,
but grew up at the sounds of drumbeats and processions, *
between believing in myths and indulging in madness.
The river cleansed our sins, often invoking fears,
leaving someone on its bed
like a plow sinks deeply to revert.
A face needs none but soon becomes the property of others.
Contradictions coexist at the desert's edge.
I stretched my hand and gathered my remains
from my spirit's ashes.
(My eyes remained transfixed on the sky's map.)
I didn't know more than the limits of what the water, the plant,
the animal, the star, the sky, the clouds' breast, and the space required.

There was no mosque or church
for the night to fathom what the dawn said,
or the light to penetrate the secrets of shades.
No sound but the echoes can be grasped by the shaking of waves,
by the smashing of the fruits on the ground,
in the language of birds and the weight of silence.
Life's seasons are complicated like the clarity of God in his absence.
What still unclear was that face, which the women's wails kicked earlier,
and the death's laughter across the fields.
Oh, yesterday, I invite you whisperingly.
You filled my mouth with sands and roses, doubts and beliefs.
What a container = + - x / . = a human being.
Wide-opened imagination and roots, closed lipped,
the agents of Highness were everywhere I passed:
in the corners and alleys, in schools, houses, and shrines,
even in the public restrooms,
but I found no one in the hearts.

I asked the *Imam* repeatedly about the movements of the spheres and lucks,
but he didn't reply.
One day, I put my hand on his window, wailed, and hit my head
on his silver rail, then, I dozed off.
I heard a hidden whimper the depths pushed toward me:
"Poverty in this land is an exile.
Richness in exile is the choice."*
Someone around me repeated:
"Zur sabos ajoshi, ba tishkir as shama dostan aziz;" **

Thank you so much my dearest friend.

When I awakened, I found me outside myself.
I was asked and still, "Where are you from?"
I was and still responded, "of nowhere."
Was a man born from nowhere?
My plow is in my hand, a handful of sand, a bouquet of flowers.
Echoes search for their source.
A poem that doesn't wish to end.

Birmingham, 4-14, 2015
Translated, Ventura, Florida Dec. 27, 2017

*A reference to *Imam* Ali's saying:

"Richness in exile is a country; poverty at home is exile."

** Farsi language

To commemorate the murder of martyr Al-Husain Bin Ali, the Shi'a walk with drums in mourning processions during the ten days of Ashura. Also, the drums were used to awaken people before dawn to eat their first meal during the month of Ramathan. People didn't have alarm clocks then. (The Translator)

Embroidering Silence

I taught myself not to trust itself
even in a dream.
Yesterday, I chewed what remained of the words' fragrance
that I forgot the savor of what I hastily swallowed.
But what scares the living, and the dead applaud,
is the profound ascension of the talk's arrow
in the cemetery of neglect.

I accustomed myself to walking at roads' edges
between the thorns and the chasms.
Someone strode on the water and the air.
The face documented me from this and that,
still carved by time, dug by bruises.
A mountain mourns a mountain.
A foothill is proud of itself.
A river fades in the depth of another.
Silence is
the only improvisor.

Jablonna, 11-30-2017
Translated: 2-7-2019

A View

I often observe my neighbors busy with their daily chores.
One plays with his Parisian cat in the garden.
Another plants more firs at his back fence.
A blond woman waters the flowers at the entrance to her house.
I assume they watch me too
through the void of the past
or a hole in the sky.
But they don't mind my wife mending her socks,
paging her days,
praying in front of the atlas of humans' destiny.
Nor do they care for me as I guard
the upcoming, collecting the roses' leaves
which the wind scattered all over the yard.

Warsaw, 7, 2, 2016

The Neighbor's Ladybug

My eighty-year-old Yiddish neighbor
hangs his straw hat on a reindeer's horn,
near the exit door's nob of two rings,
over which a picture of Christ was
shrouded by a red-white flag.
I observed him, from the house's garden,
soaking the flag and wiping Jesus's head,
putting a palm on his chest and another over the cross's hand.
Once, he told me jokingly:
"I'll invite you to the king of prohibitions."
He asks me about the East, the desert, the scorpions,
the veiled Eastern women.
If they hide anything?
Suddenly, a girl, with dancing breasts, passed by.
I said, "No divinity after now."
"We are even between nakedness and secrecy," he replied.
I asked him about the plants, the birds, the butterflies.
He beaconed, bantering, "I see you winged, my friend."
I gave him, then, at dusk, a red ladybug I found crawling
over autumn's leaves.

The work of ladybugs in nature is larger than their sizes.
They have one appearance, covered by crimson rays,
celestial stars improvising tender melodies.
Unlike mankind, whose colors are uncountable,

whose names the priest asks about on Sundays.

He continued, after silence,
"I escaped, one night, from the invaders' crematories,
the pigs' imperiousness,
changed my name to evade incineration unlike my brother and parents.
Dreaming, I was surrounded by murderers, tyrants, highway robbers.
I don't know how I survived all this distance between two extremes,
the stone's pride and a body's defeat."
My neighbor, (though a ladybug passed over his lips,)
was daydreaming of the absents' letters,
looking for his wedding band and two earrings
he presented to his wife who committed suicide.
I left him slowly drawing to the depths,
and returned hastily
to find my wife, with parted lips,
reading her fortune
from the palm of the stars.

Birmingham-Warsaw

July 22-29- 2018

Translated: 2-2-19

Barking

My Neighbor, the usurer merchant,
the claimer of faith, usurper of spring,
gatherer of offerings,
oh, this ancient man,
God's informant,
the guide of immortality, to my garden,
hammers, day and night, his nails
in the body of the space.

My neighbor, the wolf,
questioned me
about the limits of mercy and tranquility.

My dog interrupted me.
I commanded:
"Bark!"

Oh, how angelic his voice was,
the anthem of all anthems?

Jablonna, Poland, 11-10-2018
Translated: 2-2-19

Listening

I've listened enough to my shade and me.
I've eavesdropped enough on mankind.
Now, I've decided to listen to thunders and lightnings,
to the giggles of the stars,
penetrating the skull of wilderness.

Jablonna, 11-7-18
Translated 2-5-19

A Cloud

Neither the trees' moaning can be heard, nor the shaking of the walls.
The bellow was mighty; even the winds shivered fearfully.
One second collided with another;
leaves were captured, dispersing.
Suddenly, a dark cloud clanged between my feet.
If I hadn't carried out and wiped my shoe with it;
it would've spiraled over the hands, the eyes,
then ascended
to mount the shoulders and the neck.
The Flood would've been more merciful.

Dublin, 12-22-18

Translated: 2-5-2019

Harvest

The tree gifted me a bird;
I hit her with a stone.
The bird led me to the wing.
I held on the top a feather at departure.
The ants taught me drawing plans and cutting roads,
but, when I ploughed the soil,
I uprooted my ancestors' bones.

Dublin 12-29-2018

Translated: 2-5-19

Kindness

Her hair descends to the
marble cliffs of her hips.
Her eyes collect the oysters from the sea.
Her lips reveal the fortune.
Without her compassion,
I would've choked by my sighs.

Jablonna, 11-17-2018
Translated: 2-15-19

*Jasmin**

After a quarter of a century of absence,
I visited Damascus.
Jasmin covered my mother's gown.
My father's face blushed at the sight of young girls.

Twenty years later, I visited my parents' graves,
reminiscing their memories in the Levant
and their love in eternity.

* At the begging of the new millennia, invited to attend the third Meda Literary Gathering in Damascus, I took advantage to bring my parents from Iraq after 27 years of absence.

Spirits

In Baghdad,
the spirit of absent memories digs in the air.
After an abject departure, I tried to recall its shades,
but, then,
before reaching the Najat Church, *
my shoe sank in its tar.

*The Najat is one of the churches that ISIS attacked with a suicide's bomb, killing tens worshipers and maiming several more.

Hell Questions

My son asks:
"Are there prisons and gas chambers in hell, Dad,
like the ones our history teacher told us about?"
Ask your theology teacher, I replied.
"Did you forget,
I don't attend the religion session?"
Well, you should ask Isaac, our old, Jew neighbor;
he was the last to survive the civilization's crematories.
Ask your mother first.
He remarked resentfully,
"She prays, fearing hell;
all her words about it are exaggerated.
Is it possible that it fills the gap between the earth and the sky?
Its horrors are intolerable; its tenants are immortal?
Then, what is the guilt of those who stole for a piece of bread?
those plagiarized, from their classmates,
what wit and memory failed to register?
The one who drank to ease his pain?
Who revolted against a tyrant?
Who was led to sin by temptation?
And that, who sold her body to feed her hungry orphans?
Is Satan an invention of God's enemies?
Why don't you answer, Dad?"

I'm busy, my dear, I said,

patching the words, shielding the brain from rust.
Why don't you ask the Creator of Mankind?
He lowered his head
before he jabbed me with a mortal punch:

"If I had known Him, Dad,
I wouldn't have asked you."

Questions open a passage in the body.
Persuasions close the pours and deplete the oxygen.
What a strange drag,
to sow wheat and harvest fire?"

September 12, 2011

Translated: March 9, 2019

Vanity

Oh, winds, don't toy with this dust;
its grains will bloody your eyes.
And you, roses, don't hesitate to prickle my heart;
your spirit is of it;
your cheeks' rouge
is of the life flowing over its roots.

Spring's leaves fall.
Autumn's axes glitter,
but the tree's spirit is a blade
no sky limits,
no storm unveils.

I open my door to my beloved.
The winds enter, toying with the memory
of her upside picture near the window.
A kiss delayed every moment.
Two lips
over the pillow of absence
shrivel.

Spring's leaves fall.
Autumn's axes glitter,
but the tree's spirit is a blade
no sky limits,
no storm unveils.

September 20, 2011

Translated: 3-13-2019

Tearing

I planted roses and fruit trees.
At the time of harvest,
I beheld snakes nesting,
and some swine tearing
the heart of the roots.

A Harlot's Birthday

Her voice was talisman for the day's dimness.
Her eyes' radiance was a glow in the darkest calamities.
Every finger is a beacon to her history,
extending from the almonds' farm to the silk pillows
till the imagination's inception
and the burgeoning of her silence that listens and can be heard.
Without her fruits and lips' melodies,
life's inheritance would've been bleak,
and the intimacy's step stumbling.
Every grasshopper would've said,
"I'm the dove, the naughty sparrow
in the deer's oasis and the nightingales' tweet."
What a difference between a tongue's stammering and its flow.

The night was raucous.
The soft light approaching every window
which coyness's curtains altered, during the day,
into a coded page.

How many lions were tamed?
Swords sheathed and unsheathed?
Hats lifted?
Wars extinguished?
Cups were smashed over thirsty lips.
How many a dark notion was ignited by the glow of surprise?

Side by side, near the ideal cleanliness,

fulfilling our dream.
Desired:
heroic in her nudity, virtuous in her sin.
Her dreams are pure; her nights never end.

Yesterday, she extinguished her ninety.
Over her chest was a wharf where a boat recently docked.
On her back, waves, and unrequited sailors,
lightnings and thunders soothe,
and the foam disappears.

In her days' diary, an obvious and ambiguous writing
of leaders, immigrants, workers, merchants, students,
of wars' winners or losers, who write,
and then,
the trail fades away.

The bed's yawning resurrects the echo.
Her chair rocks like her age.
The candles of nine decades were snuffed
with a thousand gasps and sighs.

Alone,
she mends her tattered life.

Warsaw, May 9th, 2010

Translated: March 28, 2019

My Seven Wives

My First Wife

My wife deserted me centuries ago.
Her hair was kohl; her breast was a handful.
Her voice skated over the talk's ice.
She was the wind in my throat.
Perturbed between her dreams' loads and the agonizing life,
I remembered her yesterday,
and, over her,
I married my last wife.

My Second Wife

Every dawn, she read *Al-Fatiha* over my corpse. *
She searched for angels wafted through the clouds,
for righteous men, tracing their footprints over the dust.
Men who have formidable tombs with candles and the season of prayer.
Gabriel inhibited their souls;
they glittered for a while,
then disappeared behind the horizon.
Their spirits' light has no equivalent,
but they are the share of whim in the glorious kingdom of absence.
My wife is the honey in a mouth of a chrysanthemum.

Suddenly, the dawn shone,

inhaling from the body of despair.
Even childhood waded in ponds of blood.
Time returned to yesterday, surrendering,
and I became a flesh,
protected by the fang of mortality.

My Third Wife

A copy of the era of fire,
she wears a tent; a bundle of steel is over her back.
Her lingerie's details are designed by the school of progressive painters.
Every color has a story beyond the mind, wider than imagination's kingdoms.
She never told me her story.
(Shahrazad ended and vanished long ago.)
Outside the night, she was no more than a sigh.
My wife was a bewildered child.
I, a paper kite.

My Fourth Wife

The sky blessed her, crowning her breast with a star.
A flock of wings and suns guarded her moves.
The gods drank from her palm.
I was thirty years and one older.
Her age's laziness wasted her.
The day without an ember is a gleam of darkness.

My Fifth Wife

She has no presence other than her panting breaths.
She could be Rabab, Hind, Layla, or Fatima.
She was pure joy.
The years demeaned her as the sea humiliates its sailors.
We met in a hurry like the spring clouds.

My Sixth Wife

She is forged out of the spiders' webs.
She nags me every second with her charm.
When she is mad, I fear she would divorce me.
She has taught me to follow her trails.
My horse, invading the horizon, is a mouse.
Without a sword, a sound, or an echo,
I, the Bedouin, is jealous of her
from the promiscuous foreigner.

My Seventh Wife

A silent portrait,
she never chats or complains,
abuses or envies.
She awaits my return day and night.
Jasmin crowns her forehead.
Her love is pure.

Her breast is arrogant, shining over a false mercy.
Years passed.
I forgot the ones before her.
My wife
is a charming doll.

I was unfair; I committed suicide.
Now, I don't know
If I will go to hell
or climb
the martyrs' ladder.

January 27, 2012
Trans. May 11, 2019

**Al-Fatiha* is a verse from Qur'an for the dead.

The Camp's Letter

The shepherd's stick, masked as a sergeant,
herded thousands of dreamers of a third river in Mesopotamia.
They arrived from the universities,
but a barbarian storm returned them to the desert
to bury them alive then resurrected them so that they crawled on four,
while the daily, dry loaf was lesser than a soldier's boot
in which we repeatedly hid our ration
and the lover's photo in the sock.

The hopes were led to execution,
and the perceptions dried like dew after sunrise.
I watched my pal, Al-Mandwee, shrink every minute, *
wriggling in life's grave, from the wild glares' torment
and the tyranny of the people of the caves.
He vanquished in his prison (more merciful than his whipper)
until the personnel carriers gathered us in the road
to the storks' and the butterflies' suicide at the thresholds
of the south (of which he is an indigenous).
We forgot, behind us, what the sparrow said outside his cage,
and the mothers' hymns for our return, mixed with a dying's farewell.
Happy we were, for the first time, to see the borders as if it was eternal salvation,
no more than sapiens sand, tumbleweed, and gravel.

"Do you know, Soliman, how do the ants bury their dead
after the mares stoppled on them?

One of them crawled over my hand, pulling her sister,
but I disappointed her,
for my veins were dry; thirsty was my tongue.

Our patience lasted, my friend,
waiting for the final redemption.
We were descendants of the water's lily.
You, pigeon, return,
and, you, life
resurrects from your stones.

Birmingham, 4-29, 2018

Translated; 5-24-19

*Al-Mandwee is poet and novelist Kahtan Mahboub, Hatif's intimate friend with whom he endured a very harsh experience in the military service, first in Najaf, where Kahtan was tortured and imprisoned for writing a poem, then in the desert of Basra, in the Sixth Tank Battalion, near the Kuwaiti borders.

The Manda'ean

I don't have a bird's wing, or a dolphin's charm
to be near the hidden lapis in a Manda'ean's stream.
But I accompanied the clouds to be near The King of Light and Water. *
Yesterday, I beheld Him drunk by his gleams.

Oh, Lord of love and rain, I beseeched.
My hand wrote with my nails and even my bones what you wished.
You still guide the shades to my veranda
and the tyrant thieves to my crop.

Am I meant to stay on the land of desolation forever?
Lead me to the light behind the vision's veil.
If I thirst, cleanse my tongue.
Let the rivers' currents flow
near my door's step.

Thence, I would feed love to the hungry.
If my basket drains,
they will quench from my blood.

His clear voice reached me:
"This pure radiance will bathe the road.

A halo will cleanse its sins.

Then, a wave

from a Manda'ean spring

baptizes this being."

Birmingham, 4-22-2019

Translated: 5-24-2019

*The King of Light and Water: Mandaic, synonym for God, one of God's names in the Manda'ean religion.

Weeping Willow

She knocks on my window.
When the night arrives, I hear her moan.
She deciphers the bird's logic,
and beholds the winds like winged ships
or perplexed angels.
Her day, thus, ends
between a frown and branch's bending,
a dawn's shining and a mocking laughter of an oak tree.
If she complains, it isn't out of an ailment,
but from the meanness of her sly neighbor.

Warsaw, Feb. 22, 2013

Translated: June 16, 2019

Incomplete Seasons

I was preoccupied with surpassing a past,
burying its echo,
supporting a family
of words,
born from the womb of doubt and the incredible.
I drew a new house, with shelves, filled with books.
I had a fence, a roof, a door, and a key.
Suddenly, my heart despaired.
I found me busy
reminiscing a past, omitting its resonance.
Hence, the day ends
between what is coming
and what will never return.

Istanbul Airport, Dec. 28, 2012

Trans: June 18, 2019

Searching for The Moonlight

I used to read under the moon's light,
sometimes in the shade of a flailing lantern.
Then, I began to read the streets under the electric poles,
flipping the pages of my life, in a city
shielding its face during the day,
baring its thighs after dark.

Then, I entered Baghdad.
I beheld it submerging in mud,
and someone builds his life
by chopping his passing neighbors.

The lost city's clothes glitter.
Beauty envies its women;
its nights were insomniac with joy.
I was unmasking the stranger's code,
searching for the spring's alphabet.

Tell me: oh, fires, streets, seasons,
and you, tattered bones,
why, after all these sacrifices,
I couldn't find my homeland?

What fates designed wasn't what the vision
and the fortune palms read.

I regretted all I wrote in the past.

What I loved was smashed under the horses' hoofs,
and absence tramped over its breasts.

Our escape was an imposed circle.
Now, the family, the air, the water,
the datepalms, memories, words, and we all
became exile that begs us to rejuvenate its blood circle
after the monster locked his jaws
in the land of betrayal and death,
stifling the neck of the alphabet.

We pray for the clouds,
for our trees began to grow in the void.
Perhaps this is the only solution to defeat
what we still reminisce.

In the past, I used to hope for the coming
with the mirror of spring.
Today, I gather autumn's scattered grains.

Oh, prophecies, stars, and you, fortunetellers,
answer me, is what we have seen,
what you predicted?

September 6th, 2011

Translated: June 18, 2019

Is it Too Late? *

Returning dreaming to our families,
we beheld, in front of the houses,
signs of unrest, complaint, and our brothers dismayed.
We asked; no one said "hello," or "welcome,'
to these masses of expatriates.

We saw soldiers, dead, wailing, and chest beating,
jamming our way to complain to Ali,
what happened yesterday and today:
"Can we be oppressed by your constituents
such and such and such,
and, we are your sons,
of the conscience which shies to moan
or bare the face to appease the sinners,
the falsifiers from the jurist sultans.

Were our tears, the mountains, the deserts, we crossed
only lightning to the rulers
who laugh in the morning and cry in the evening
in front of their bread givers of conniving emperors?

When we returned, we found our loved ones,
from the cells' comrades and days of affection,
before the exiles,
are the assassins.

Why do we return then?
Is it to our fate, to close a circle
between our departure
and, now, the spawning blood
of the Two Rivers' corpse? **

Why did we return remorseful to our families?
Oh, my spirit's dove,
the swords' blades in Hussein's chest,
answer me?

Warsaw, August 12, 2011.
Translated, June 18, 2019

*After 35 years of escaping and fighting the dictatorship, its descendants request us to show proof of the political harms we suffered to return to our previous services.

** Tigris and Euphrates

A Lover's Message to His Beloved

In the Est,
they found a strange script
belonging to two lovers:

"Your dreams, striding in my body,
are life's nectar which we together inhaled.
Your soul beats in my veins.
My morning begs for the warmth of your yesterday,
shining in the heart of darkness.
I breathe the air like an incinerator.
I'm the existent, about to be mortified.

The last wish for your voice,
arriving from a distance,
smothering the crossing torch for the other shore,
where the butterfly traces the light's trail,
hovering
over a blind lantern.

Spring awakens inside us, my friend.
The strides rejoice.
The hands entangle with the roots,
and the ribs with the branches
in the partnership of the trip,
gifted to intimacy.

Do you know Enkidu and Gilgamesh?
The snake, flicking its tongue behind the horizon,
after cunningly stealing,
the plant of eternity?

We were friends too.
Ah, what a final journey,
searching for the puzzle of immortality.

Is beauty dull?
Is love pervert?
Are our hopes vain?
Was our meadow meant to bathe in thunderstorms?
Are flowers sinful?

Our affection's history is heavy,
but its treasure is life's shine,
and hope's gleam.

My friend,
I've seen your innocent boat departing;
the waves cradle;
the foams follow.

That was the apple of our youth,
fell into the sand of the East,

and the ants swarming after."

Oh, friendship, as you wave
to the last boat in the river of despair,
someone, in the road to you,
leaves the door open to doubts' ax
while, at the curb, they found your golden hair's comb
and the remains of your broken mirror.

May 29, 2009

Translated: August 4, 2019

*This poem is dedicated to the youths who were murdered in the East by the pretext of deviation and homosexuality.

Death Dance

I received adds about burial, its procedures,
and the heirs' rights
though I am borrowing my sustenance
from the mouth of the abyss.
I repeatedly deleted all,
closed my account, and relaxed.
But they remembered me again
after the events In Iraq.
Once more, my mail was jammed.
I said, I must write to the Supreme Leader.
"My God," I addressed Him.
"Be merciful even once with me.
My blood spawns in the roads.
My spirit is dangling over autumn's branch,
agonizing.
My mail is full with the names of the fallen.
My God, this is not my time, please.
Remove your informants from my life's file."

Birmingham, 10-27-19
Translated: 1-9-20

Cesar Vallejo's Dream

Huascaran shouldn't have left me all these years*
roaming between exile and a hunger's frown.
Sitting in front of a scene partially shrouded by clouds,
dangling from the pockets of the sky,
I glanced myself in a passing moment, climbing a hill
tripping every step by my sigh,
and the height I overcame began to disappoint me
breaking a rib or two.
Suddenly, I heard a knock at the window.
A flower extended to me from the hand of the void
with a note attached to its neck:
"Congratulation for your new grave."
I haven't died yet, in Paris, I yelled,
though I perished numerously before in my homeland.
I am still at the beginning of the road.
This blood, spilling around me,
is only lovers' hymn.

Birmingham, 1-10-2019
Translated: 1-9-20

* Huascaran is the highest mountain in Puro

*Dreaming of Shetha**

Perhaps fortunes, at the crossroads, reconcile,
and the consultations, before the first spark, be near.
I whispered to one of them
that perhaps a breeze of you,
hailed by the winds, brings me the seed of the promise.
Thus, I will be spared a dialogue over life's destiny,
and the stealing of a foolish glimpse
from humans' living.

It is not disgraceful then for hopes to chase what is ambiguous.
A glow of beauty may seek refuge
in a fading light, on a forlorn road,
in ruins crowned by the flowers of the prairies.
I ascended by a vision of a dream turned into reality
penetrated by dawn's rays,
so that my life swims in the flame.

You are silent like a meadow in the heart of spring.
But you don't know
that the airs, the thunders, the constellations:
languages of mortality's fear,
are still dreaming of returning
to your lips.

Yablona, 7-8-2018

Translated: 109-2020

*Shetha is the poet's wife.

A Homeland's Mirror

The informants in my homeland
are more merciful than snakes,
more compassionate than a dagger in the back.

They hold the keys to paradise
and the first glow of igniting the universe.
They don't know weeping;
they learned to dry the tears before they fall
rain from the eyes of others.
They always suffice by a faint smile
as they ich their scalps and rear-ends.

The informants in my homeland are humble.
They sympathize with the ruins and absences.
They adore the black, stained by red,
greeting with one finger on the trigger,
beckoning, with the other, toward the cliff.

One day, I passed by a temple with open doors.
I beheld a swath of hair attached to a shoe's sole.
Then, I noticed a scarlet shirt under a book.
Since then, I've been following the ant of suspicion,
watching the silencer's mouth,
counting what it may reveal to me of sighs.

Yablona: 2-4-2019
Translated: 1-14-2020

Sigmund Freud's Labyrinth

We look upward; he glares at the depth.
There, from the underworld, he writes the will.
We, in an exciting show, copy our suicide,
upset with him; he reminds us of our nakedness.
We dream of planets and females.

He said to life: "I wasn't permitted to die.
Now, I've the right to."*
But he didn't die
even from a kiss in a harlot's lap.
He remained dangling on the branch of compassion, **
thinking of love and death.
One hand tucked into a pocket;
the other appears to be tickling death from above
as lost comets do.

Like this, we die, every minute,
naked, as a scale,
living as a snail,
dreaming of harlots, agonizing.
To sweep what has settled in the stream's bed,

we deeply hide love's only oyster;
and, on the stone of the delayed mystery,
break the residue.

Yablona 1-5-2019
Jan. 20th, 2020

*This is what Freud said after the death of his mother.

**This is a reference to the statue of Sigmund Freud by David Cerny in Old Prague.

Cerny depicted Freud dangling from an overhang ledge with one hand while the other is tucked in his pocket.

Agony

A veil is on her breast,
wine spills on the cliff.
The light smiles behind her hair,
and I read the verse of the universe
in her book.

Warsaw 1-12-2019

1-20-2020

Memory's Ash

Oh, soil,
is the blood of sacrifices insufficient for you?
We are also from clay and water.

Oh, dust, halt.
Your atoms prick the roses' eyes.
We are too from the texture of butterflies.
Oh, meadow beatifies,
for the datepalm's pollen of Sumer
smeared the faces, from the first inception,
bathing in the nights' wine,
awakening at the dew's smile,
drank by the night's breast's kiss.

Oh, soil
we are from you.
You are
not from us.

Yablona 3-3-2019

Jan. 19, 2020

Floating Islands

Sitting,
the days are beneath a wall in my back.
In the eyes' window,
the trees grow; the ants seem occupied,
weaving their mazes,
and the beaks, in their nests, call for rescue.
But the sky still knits the yarn of absence.
Nature's wound is deep,
caressed by the winds, mended by the trail.

My wife suddenly entered, murmuring:
"The flies came early.
The weather is proper to mow the grass,"
she went on.
I shook my head, drowning,
where the muse licks the clouds.

Spring arrived flailing.
I beheld some withered branches,
and a year after year,
the weeds gnawed the flowers and the scent.

"Don't sleep," my wife says.
What you see is a concurrent scene

at a time crushed by dusk
on a Sunday morning
while the clouds are floating islands
in the sky.

Yablona 5-8-2011
1-20-2020

Situations

I still suspect myself, fearing for my neighbor from it.
I plant flowers in front of the garden
and put their beds where a passerby can see.
I style my hair's remainder with the last mode.
The other's mirror wounds.
I mingle with my birthday, unknown to me,
so that my wife's friends and family accept,
and poetry's mermaids smile to me.
Poetry needs coquette and femininity.
Rhythm is an utmost necessity.
I still score goals here and there,
proud of beating Messi and Ronaldo. *
I polish my shoes every day with two spits
and beat the sidewalk's forehead.

I avoid the hatred of those I love
that I forget myself.
I've no infinite existence,
a celestial creature,
the air breathes me.
The water drinks me.
My strides pull me.
My words guide me.

The wine is mixed with the blood.

My words,

for they wrote me,

I became more perplexed than a nail

penetrating my flesh.

Birmingham, August, First, 2016

Translated: Dec. 31, 2020

*Two famous soccer players (The Translator)

Windmill

Life is sand blown by memories,
an interrupted melody listening to the drumbeats.
Between a night and its noon, the eyelashes fell on the grass.
The eyelids were tied to hopes rooted in the mountains' heights,
whereas beneath the summit, there was a pasture,
cottages over which vultures hovering,
and a tribe of mermaids.

What is life then?
Is it a flag to be raised till the day of judgement
while I, out of its fiber, a thread yarned by time?
How can a thread invent itself, loaming its rug again?
Does it, in this doom, create a third road,
or is it a rock, rolling from the top of the sky?

The absent has an excuse like the present has a stab.
Waves push waves.
A lung breathes another;
a windmill looks at the field
with the eyes of a stone mill.

The Spoon

Every empty spoon,
pretending to be full, reminds me
of the starving's agonies.

I ask it,
what leads the meal to desire the freshness of meat,
dividing, then shredding it
with a grudge and a hidden malice?

But because spoons are spiritless,
having no players' dominance,
they can't be reprimanded or reply.
Yet, their silliness and hollowness,
led me to doubt their usefulness,
to hammer the table with my fist,
that the knives fell on my side.

There was a scooper,
a fork,
a wail.
I wasn't a hero;
thus, I retreated, humble, and upset.

Every empty spoon

has a knife, a fork, a companion
a cry of hunger behind its back,
and another sated to its neck.

Every empty spoon
drowned
in my blood.

Warsaw, June 2000
Revised and translated Jan, 6. 2020

Absence

Absence, extending beyond its shadow,
still stars at us with half-shut eyes.
It won't be this wide
if its road is trodden,
visible, or a scowl above its eyebrows.

Absence, without a scent,
has no dew or a flare,
yet a captivating dominance.
Am I who promised the roses with spring,
the valleys and mountains with echo,
bridging the gap between the grass and the stone,
the visible and the invisible?
Am I who weaved its soaked yarn,
framing it by the cunning of mirrors
the widows' wailings, the fire's flames,
and with the hand, shining in the air,
coding, blessing it with henna,
staining it with blood?
Am I...?

"Absent«
I wrote on my forehead:
"don't look for me:
I am a rare melody sang by time

to my idle of life foes
and the forgotten dead."
I welted as a whispering tune at the drums' margins,
in roads I trekked alone.
Others are on hold behind the walls of the day,
reading its tilted coffee cup
with cloudy eyes and shivering hand
in a space weaved by oblivion,
by the string of the perfidious virtue.

Near the beloved, I espy
a light fading behind the hills.
Suddenly, she silenced like the dusk,
her neck bleeding, glittering,
in the pages of darkness.

Absence equals absence;
how much light in it and dimness?

Only this loss,
at the ladder's cliff
can decode absence's talisman
extending in the memory.

Warsaw 9-5-2008
Jan. 24, 2020

The Beetle

Aristotle was skilled in depicting them such.
But, because he was a historian without wings,
he never imagined their enormous numbers,
and twice more for those who lost them,
and manufactured them hundreds of years later.

He saw the beetle crawling,
but missed the bright side of the very wing,
busy then with the epic of the human's night,
by the drama of the wingless.
Are their legs by couples or multiples?
Does their spirit walk, crawl, or fly?

Only the night doesn't separate those of the wing
and those who dream of it.
Both turn their head and body
at the crossroads;
the one with two feet; the other with many.
The first despises darkness, for he always creates it;
the other doesn't see it, finding no oddity in its form,
or a deformity in its silence.
The beetles aren't all scarabs to flip on their backs.
The winged doesn't trip by darkness;
ignite a lamp,
or extinguish a candle.

She, encased in black, buries her dead
and weeps for the rest of her life.

The scarab is the Pharos's amulet,
bluer than the East's sky,
carved like the Nile on time's body;
neither the tender chests nor the dead's habits
are of it afraid.

Aristotle is an expert in tracing the human's shade.
With a white scarf, the dream's flag,
his head rotates in every direction,
searching for a lantern and a wing,
in the kingdom of darkness:
the flying, the crawling,
even in the unattainable shades.

Warsaw, April 20, 2018
February 15, 2020

Aristotle thought that a human can understand himself by examining the nature of the living creature and their natural habitat. He, therefore, studied more than five hundred kinds of animals and insects, among which was the beetle.

The Raven

Rainy, and the winds turn the spaces into sirens:
gems, scattering in every direction.
A raven perched by my window;
an evil omen in the East,
despite the love in his season, his strife,
and the great symbol, seeking salvation and escape.

I am not a god or a flood survivor
to bring him down from his highness.
I don't wish ravens crow at the doors,
or mothers pray for healing.
Every day I steal the offerings of the deities.
I don't wish the ravens to lead me to victory then crumple at my feet
as if I am an old man sitting among the preys.

I saw a raven with a branch in his beak,
whose glares are so fierce even darkness fears.
A few of his feathers dimmed the window's gleam,
touching my mouth.
I said to him: "Oh, you, robber of the light from the sky.
I've returned from death, my friend,
but my loved ones didn't.

What is happening?

Why every second the dream commits suicide?"

Yesterday, a raven stood at my window,

with a wheat stalk in his beak.

I didn't see him today.

Birmingham, December second, 2015

Translated: February 15, 2020

A Wish

I fear for my wish from the living and the dead.
I unveil it to the ears of the inanimate:
the chair, the table,
the cup and it perturbed spirit.
I observe the flowers carrying their corollas,
yet, with their petals, they glare a fluttering bee.
I reveal my perplexity to the shades
which no longer fathom my opaqueness
or decipher the code of dusk.
What remains
is to unfold my wish to the thunder and the abyss,
write it over a bird's wing
and release it to the horizon and the wind.

Birmingham: February 8, 2020

Translated: February 15, 2020

The Iraqi Hunchback

Perturbed,
he carries over his shoulders
the travels of Sumer, Ashore, and Babylon.
His life is a swing between the summit and the abyss.
His luck is weaker than a spider's strand.
His back suddenly bent
over the eclipse's blade.
Step by step, he vanishes
like a beam of light in the heart of dusk.
The arrow shoots from his lungs,
from the highest summit behind him,
but, for now, he doesn't know
if this is a mere sigh, piercing the sky,
or is it the arrow uprooting his heart?
like an expanding flame
toward the dreamers' realm.

Birmingham, Jan. 29, 2020
Feb. 8, 2020

Return

I return to what the heart should do
without a burden, a macabre
a wailing, or a fuss.
I kiss a rose and pity a cloud.
Heavy-headed, I glare at this life
like a spike of wheat.

Birmingham, 1-22-2020

Translated: Jan. 28-2020

Homeland

A shiver quaked my body.
Seeking the cause,
I found the lips closed
over a homeland,
at the dusk of the Arabs,
devoured by death.

The Bark's Eulogy

I call upon you from life's depth
from its seething, agony, perplexity, and white core,
from a branch dangling under the weight of rain,
from my spirit's fruits, falling on the ground,
and my hairdo, messed up by the wind.
Oh, sunrise, the bird, the storm,
I call you to say goodbye,
and, oh, naughty bark,
spring's guard
in the heart of retreat.

Birmingham 1-23-2020

1-28-2020

The Wind's Grasp

I will leave you tomorrow or the day after,
and say what is needed to be said.
My language is the thunders; my home is the sparks.
I will undoubtedly depart in a wink,
but will remain, to the end,
the wind's grasp in the storm.

Birmingham 10-11-2019

Translated Jan. 28, 2020

I Am the Wind

They complain of missing the beloveds' kiss,
cleansing the deceased, dressing them the shroud of absence,
burying them respectively.
They shrivel like them, a sound in the valley,
as if they arrived from oblivion.

Women in scarfs crowned with blackness.
Tears fallen from the sieve of distance
over the grains of dust,
the flowers wilted in the road.

Ulysses returned but not Monteverde, *
a halo, guarded by hilltops, awaiting him.
The hymns are forlorn in the Lioness of the Country. **
Cerberus still wails at its gate,
and the words were cast over the pain's question.

Do you hear me Marcelo Peralta from the depth of this dimness? ***
And you, oh, Luis Sepulveda****
was *The Oldman Who Read Love Stories*,
still prays so that you immerge from your magic lamp?

How can distance listen to the tune's beat,

to life's pulse between the lips?
Can they close over a thirsty kiss
while the valleys are full of fogs?

The falling rocks mislead the returnees,
searching for those who drank
the wine of separation from the palm of fate.
They have no graves;
only the crowned with the dull sickle
hovers over the fields.

The womb's smile on the newly born's lip,
these lilies at the mountains' sides
will omit the sudden departure.

Every moment I mourn the wing's breakage,
where the bird carries to the nest
a bite to his chicks.
I wrestle the trees and the roots,
to remove the remainder
of dry leaves
over the branches' charms.

I am the wind resurrected from the abyss,
unveil the treasure embroidered with hearts.

I am the wind lifting the sales,
the secret captivating the storm,
the w…i…n…d.
I am the air searching for shelter
in the lungs' inhale.

Yablona 4-12-2020
Translated 5-7-2020

*Claudio Monteverdi (1567-1643) was one of the main founders of the Italian opera, best known for conducting the anthem choir at the Basilica of San Marco in Venice. "Return of Ulysses" is among his most famous operas.

** Poet Giosuè Carducci (1835-1907) called Brescia the "Italy's Lioness," a city in the region of Lombardy that was highly affected by Coronavirus.

***Marcelo Peralta (March 1961 - March 2020) an Argentine musician and saxophonist fell victim to Coronavirus in Madrid.

****Luis Sepúlveda (1949 -16 April 2020) Chilean writer died infected with Coronavirus. *The Old Man Who Reads Love Stories* and *"Aladdin's Magic Lamp"* are some of his works.

Simulating the Bird at the Time of Corona

The bird's logic is the noblest.
The wind's rustle; the thunder, the lightning nurtured it.
The silent sings; the listener mutes.
People's gossip hurts him,
and when we fly away, flapping,
tenderness in his chirping
melody in his echo,
we chant at his tune.
We failed in our arithmetic stride until the voice repulsed.
We built an isthmus for our life from the sun's sigh,
having the saw's and the ax's habit
to chop the forest to rubbles
at the sunsets' wakes
and the shivering of the dew.

Emboldened by the night,
we demolish what was built by toils and tears,
smelling the nectar of lips.
When we agonize,
we hide behind the virtues of the breast.

We doze off at the day's lull, dreaming of a paradise
ascending by a borrowed wing,
then sink
in the horizon's ambiguities.

Yablona, 4-10-2020

Translated 5-7-2020

Gratitude

Thank you forests and prairies
for resembling my spirit in its divergences.
Thank you, mountains for enduring the burdens,
seeing the visions before anyone else.

Thank you, ancient sand for loving the rain,
the electric wires for enduring,
oh, women, for shielding your husbands' genitals,
and you, children of the East,
for bearing your parents' sins.

Thank you datepalm of the half-mast flag,
mourning a land,
vanishing in the landfills of memory.

Thank you flowers for being neutral,
the winds for chasing the trail.
Thank you, streets for coping with so many shoes,
hearing the empty words.

Thank you, Sun, for staying awake,
cemeteries for housing so many dead,
and you, ants, for not crawling
on what remained of the ailing soul.

Thank you, nightmares, more compassionate than the politicians.
Oh, birds, for coloring a sky, abandoned by God,
betrayed by prophets and its people.

Thank you, tombs of Saints and Imams
for coping with people's callousness and hallucination.
You, words, for not deceiving me,
the muse, for not drying yet,
the exile, for not gnawing me yet,
and the remainders of my friends
despite all temptations.

Thank you, oh, two bleeding rivers,
for standing firm, still alive.

Thank you, death.
You are too late.

Warsaw, 2-26-2013

Translated 1-10-2019

Hatif Janabi

Author

Born in Iraq, in 1951, poet Hatif Janabi holds a B.A in Arabic literature from the University of Baghdad, M.A and a Ph.D. from The University of Warsaw in comparative theater. He is a unique, talented poet with a sharp vision and a philosophical mind. His love for his homeland and freedom is unequivocal. His poems are modern in their forms and subject matters, singing for the beauty of nature, people, and the love of life, challenging evil in all its forms, defending human rights. The poet enjoys a wide presence in world literary arenas; his poems are translated to several languages.

Kahtan Mahboub

Translator

"Poet of the Sun, Exile, and Liberty," novelist, translator, Kahtan Mahboub was born in Iraq in 1950. He holds a B.A in English and French from The University of Baghdad,1972; M.A. in English and creative writing, from WMU, Kalamazoo, MI, 1978, and a Ph.D. in American Literature and creative writing from IUP, Indiana University of Pennsylvania. His dissertation, *The Role of the Psychohistorical Heritage on the Behavior and Fate of the Individual in Faulkner's Writings*, was published in 1983. His compassionate poetry sings for love, freedom, nature, his homeland, and fights for justice and peace. He published several volumes of poetry, a novel, and a biography, in English and Arabic. His poems are translated to many languages. Dr. Kahtan Mahboub has been teaching English, creative writing, and world literature for 45 years, and at Macomb Community College, Michigan, for the last 20 years. .